Anger Control

Understanding Anger And How To Deal With Your Anger Issues Easily

❖

Chris Porter

DISCLAIMER

This information is provided and sold with the knowledge that the publisher and author do not offer any legal or other professional advice. In the case of a need for any such expertise consult with the appropriate professional. This book does not contain all information available on the subject. This book has not been created to be specific to any individual's or organizations' situation or needs. Every effort has been made to make this book as accurate as possible. However, there may be typographical and or content errors. Therefore, this book should serve only as a general guide and not as the ultimate source of subject information. This book contains information that might be dated and is intended only to educate and entertain. The author and publisher shall have no liability or responsibility to any person or entity regarding any loss or damage incurred, or alleged to have incurred, directly or indirectly, by the information contained in this book.

Thank you for downloading this book. Please review on Amazon for us so that I can make future versions even better. A portion of the proceeds from this book goes to American Cancer Society®. Thank you for you support. God bless.

Just for Downloading this book and showing your support, I wanna give you 2 of our other books, absolutely **FREE**. Just go to the link and subscribe and get **2 Free Books** for your support. Don't forget to give us **5 star Rating** so we can make better versions to help more people. Thank you guys for your support.

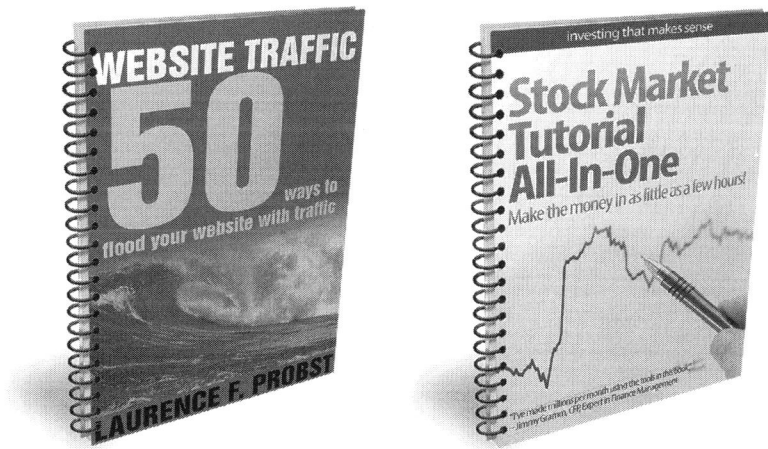

Click Here to Download-Free **Website Traffic & How To Invest in The Stock Market**

Table of Contents

Foreword

Angriness may be an issue in your every day life if you let it be. Not only does it interrupt your work and play, but it may hurt you when you least anticipate it. Anger has an underhanded way of making itself known in the rarest of situations, and most you do not have any control over.

Some of the times individuals don't even know that they're angry till something occurs to touch off the sudden alteration in mood. If this has happened to you, you might feel that there's no way to repair your fundamental problem as you don't understand where it comes from.

This is just not true. This book may help you to recognize what anger is, why you're going through the emotion in the first place, and what you are able to do to keep it from wrecking your life.

Utilizing this book as a guide to repairing your anger issues you might discover yourself in the midst of the problem, you might find that something in your past that you have no command over still rules your emotions now.

How To Deal With Your Anger Issues Easily.

Chapter 1:

Dread and Negativism

Synopsis

Fear is the chief fundamental source of all anger. If you've trouble managing your anger, dread is most likely the source of your issue. When you discover how to deal with fearfulness you're taking a huge leap toward commanding your life. Utilizing rational self talk strategies is among the better solutions for addressing fear itself. If negative thinking is a component of your every day life you are able to easily alter your frame of mind by abiding by some tips.

Looking Deeper

Negative thinking aims your attitude into the incorrect direction and frequently raises an individual's chance of going off when anger builds up. Individuals who refuse to seethe positive in life are generally shallow. If you think that you're hopeless, you'll always have issues added to your every day life.

Being an "if" individual, will likewise set you up for failure. Postulating "what if this occurs", or "what if that," may lead to irrational fear. You ought to keep your mind in the correct place to see to it that you don't amass any unneeded concerns. Pay attention to the matters you are able to alter and leave the matters you can't alter alone. Don't waste your time questioning and worrying about something you know you've no effect on.

There's no need to fret about the matters in the past. Keep your thoughts unclouded and you'll be less likely to build up fear.

A few individuals set themselves up for blasts of anger by questioning something that occurred weeks ago. Let yourself be free from the pressure of past instances as you can't undo anything that's already been done. You ought to learn to value what you do have command over, instead of stress yourself out about the situations that you don't. If you've trouble arriving at decisions, then you're just like the remainder of us. We all have issues making the correct conclusions in life, and that doesn't mean that the world has to topple. What it means is that you ought to take the correct steps to settle the issue.

- assess the issue cautiously

- survey your choices for resolving the issue

- take out your resources to deal with the issue

- gather up the necessities needed to solve the issue

- Come to a absolute decision

- Take steps to treat the problem right away

Putting matters off only makes things worse. Arriving at a good decision will be proven by a profitable outcome. Make sure to pat yourself on the back for a task well done.

Anger may be damaging or positive. When you discover yourself furious you might often walk off from the issue or deal with it by shouting at the source. The emotion of anger may either control us or drive us to succeed in life. If your mind is filled up with negative thoughts you'll most likely burst when a threat strikes your emotions.

A few of us convey anger through hitting, slapping, verbally attacking, mentally maltreating, punching walls and other surfaces to let your anger out. Nothing but hurt comes from these activities. Striking or slapping somebody will leave you in the slammer or leave the victim in the hospital. Striking an individual leaves emotional scars that will stay on for years. Also, punching walls, glass, and furniture may induce harm to yourself. It makes no common sense to act negatively or noxiously when you're angry.

Many times your emotions will play pranks on your brain. Many times you might get angry because you sense that somebody made you look foolish in the situation. This is only self abasement and it's a blind alley. Occasionally you might have issues understanding what somebody is saying. The best thing to do is to decelerate and ask for an explanation from the individual. This often beams a light on the state of affairs and you might be surprised to discover that the individual wasn't trying to endanger your emotions in any way.

Many persons feel threatened by individuals that don't listen to them when they're talking. You might ask yourself if you're imagining the situation or if no one truly hears you. It's good to speak up when you're being menaced by another, but it is not a great idea to respond in a harsh manner that won't solve the issue. Behaving in anger will only harm yourself and the others around you. You'll only be adding more troubles to your life and everybody else's around you.

Individuals are much less likely to hear your side of the story and will often loose regard for you when you act in such a manner. You can't blame other people for your behaviors or actions, so the regard you lose will be your blame as you responded with immaturity when you were angry.

If you can't determine a way to check your anger, find somebody that you trust to help you command your overflowing emotions. Somebody else might be able to talk you out of your angriness. Many individuals with anger issues utilize their energy in other ways, like volunteering. This way, your energy is spent in a fertile manner rather than a tempestuous one. You may offer your expertise in a particular area to help other people or youngsters to better themselves. Joining a gymnasium to relieve frustration soften a good idea.

Chapter 2:

Drug Abuse And Anger

Synopsis

Addressing your anger is grueling enough. When you impart drug abuse it may compound your existing disease. Individuals with issues with alcohol and drugs frequently feel that the world has let them down. They might have issues with stress, anger, and self-regard. Most head to the liquor store when they feel anger spring up, this may add to their issue by making the feelings acuter.

Extra Problems

Boozing and using drugs adds to the feeling by presenting them no control over their issues. You'd be well served to discover a more productive technique to deal with the tension your life brings you and the anger that comes with it.

Turning to intoxicants and drugs ought to never be a choice for dealing with tension. After freeing your life of substances like alcohol and drugs you'll be on your way to mending the problem. Only once you quit using will you be able to grapple with your anger and frustrations and finally defeat its hold on your life.

These drugs might affect your mind-set on the world and cause anger issues:

• Speed

• Pot

• Alcohol

• Ecstasy

• Cocaine

• Ephedrine

- Caffeine

- Methamphetamine

- Heroine

- Xanex

- Valium

Most likely you've lived a life with developmental defects in your personal growth, including lack of educational knowledge that helps you to view matters in full light. If you hail from a family with such issues you might not know any better than to turn to intoxicants and drugs for any problem that makes itself known in your life.

You might have learned from an early age that to deal with matters you have to turn inward. Either your parents or an adult role model of healthy anger management weren't around to teach you the right way to cope with your anger and frustration. You are able to teach yourself all the same, but first you must confront it full on.

You might even have mental illness that's keeping you from having a generative lifestyle. Adding alcohol and drugs is just a different problem that you don't need to bring to your existence. Utilizing your resources will show you that there are medicines that may help you deal with mental illness and the frustrations that issue forth from it. You'll notice there are additional options like help groups and anger management classes to teach you a much better way of coping with your stress and anger.

In a lot of instances problems are added to people's lives pulled from their own behavioral issues. Alcohol induces a loss of inhibitions causing you to convey your emotions freely without preservation. Since your percepts, sound and words are all affected, you might misconstrue something said to you. This might cause you to burst out in anger and possibly get into a conflict. Believing that alcohol and drugs are the solution to your troubles leads you down a road to total devastation. Life is full of troubles that we all have to face daily. The mystery is learning how to deal with the issues that will enhance your success and power to cope.

Chapter 3:

Being Depressed

Synopsis

Depression may lead to unrestrained anger. Taking charge of your emotions produces prompt results for the better. Depression might be the fundamental cause of most of your anger problems, and what is worse is that you might not know any better. You might require a screening for depression that might be done in your local hospital or doctor's office.

Being Blue

Depression screenings in your region might even be a free people service offered on a regular basis. When you understand that your anger isn't in your control, you are able to take the steps to healing yourself of it permanently. If you're in need of medicine or treatment the doctor's in your region will help you to discover the best possible assistance they can give you. With the assistance of the doctors in your region you might be on your way to improving yourself and your life.

There are additional types of personality disorders that might be the cause for your anger:

- Depression

- Manic depressive illness

- Insomnia

- Schizophrenia

- Anxiety

- Post-partum disorders

Take the steps essential to get yourself checked over medically. It may save you your life. Existing in a life with anger is like living without fun and love. There's no way to be in a sound relationship and to achieve your goals with such a big issue in the way. Once you've healed yourself of your depression you are able to be on your way to a spick-and-span life without the anger problems in your past and recognize that life is too short to remain angry.

As noted earlier, life is too short to fret about the matters you can't control. If you're clambering to reach the goals you've set for your life, you might want to split your goals down into littler feats and work slowly to accomplish each one. Goals set reasonably relieve your mind and body of tension making it simpler to get to your target. Take time every day to indulge yourself. Check into coping relaxation reaction strategies that leave both your mind and body benefited.

Feeling deluged is something we all go through. Take a minute to inhale and out for 10 counts. Cuddling up on the couch and popping in your pet movie will benefit your brain as you'll be letting your thoughts go. Train yourself to center on what you're doing, rather than bothering with what you're not. These strategies will clear your mind and make unwinding much simpler. You'll most likely have troubles for the rest of your life if you open yourself to anger. Take charge of your emotions and don't let depression set you off.

Depression will play pranks on your brain, occasionally as a result of a chemical imbalance you can't control. There's no reason to not visit your physician to rule this out from your causes for anger. You'll likewise learn more about depression and anxiety on your visit with your physician and you are able to discover a way to gain command of your life once again.

Chapter 4:

Anger Influences

Synopsis

Anger may be molded by friends, family, or others that you might have come into contact with throughout your life. The way we cope with our anger differs in all instances. You might be angry about something in your life that you can't master or something in the here and now that you've no way of tackling, but how you cope says a lot about your rearing and your life growing up. When you see illustrations of how things should be dealt with in your daily life you should make certain they're good ones.

Influences

When you're young you don't understand the difference between a great way to cope with anger and a foul way, it is not till you're much older that you begin to determine the difference. When you see somebody cope with a situation with poise and integrity try and integrate that into your life-style. The next time something like this arises you'll comprehend how to handle the situation in a respectful fashion. This might take some time and work on your part, but you'll be taking the measures essential to recover from your anger issues.

It's really hard to go through life without being angry at something or somebody at one time or some other. The mystery is learning to cope with your anger and discovering how to effectively declare your anger without inducing harm. For instance, if you're dealing with a person that's quite self-opinionated in a matter you might take offense to, the most beneficial thing to do is alter the subject or to kill them with kindness.

Altering the subject when you begin to feel angry may save you time and energy in the long-term. You should always alter the issue if possible, but if it isn't try and talk about something nice about the individual talking or add something nice about the matter. It's hard to persist in your downward conversation while somebody is lifting it up with courteous words; all they can do is pause and wonder about you and what you're saying. Perhaps they even wonder if they're wrong about the matter completely.For instance, when somebody is discussing a particular political view or politic you happen to be fond of in a sense that angers you, say something about the individual they favor or the individual you favor that's nice and unexpected. It will throw them off totally and you'll be saved from your wrath. There's nothing to become angry about any longer and you get to feel good for stopping yourself before you begin on an angry spell. You'll feel invigorated and will have learned something about the next time you get into a spot that's making you angry. You are able to take your first experience and supplement it. In time you'll know how to handle positions before they come about. It will be a relief recognizing that you're in command of your emotions.

Chapter 5:

What Anger Accomplishes

Synopsis

Angriness plays the leading role in domestic violence events. Individuals who abuse their spouse are in this spot and angry due to an antisocial upset underlying in their mind. Anger is the leading symptom of personality disorders like paranoid schizophrenia, asocial personality, psychopathic, sociopath, etc. Antisocial conduct personalities are part of most of the individuals in abusive relationships as well as other things....

What Happens

This sort often assaults when their guard is down like when they're under the influence or booze. They've been known to brush aside rules and regulations as they feel they're authorized to do so. Asocial personality types are highly controlling and by not conforming to their say-so you'll be left as a vent for their anger in a vehement manner. This sort of person has never been a demonstrated candidate for recovery; meaning individuals that batter their spouses will most likely carry on till somebody dies. It is not sensible to engage in these states of affairs because a chance of hope is uncommon.

Finally, demise will frequently become the focus during the beating.

Finally somebody will die, as the person's anger will grow through the years. They'll seldom invite help and even in getting it, frequently fail. Standing back from relationships that include such a personality would be good. A few of the signs to look for would be crazed looks or expressions, laughing for no evident reason, finding humor in a state of affairs when a individual was harmed, or anger bursts for no reason.Behind shut doors is when the marauder comes out even though they'll frequently lead you to believe that he or she is an example for society. Deep-rooted jealousy is another anger issue with these types of persons. They go past their limit of alcohol ingestion only increasing the odds of them blowing up in rage. Anger is frequently ignored over a long course of time. That's when anger may kill. When an individual is overly angry he has the inability to convey his anger without blowing up. That's when you know that the issue needs prompt attention. Alcohol and drugs are not involved in all instances but will stir up the already burning fire into oblivion. Hatred is the root of all anger and the individual with issues often has a difficult time checking his or her impulses, wants and emotions. Acting out of whim, the individual often assaults the source of his anger. Not everybody decides to commit murder when they've an anger issue but in a few cases it's happened and will happen over again.

Self talk may be a good way to express anger. You may want to ask yourself what is going on in your mind when you're losing control. The anger might be built within for years, or it may be caused by the now, you are able to start analyzing your mind when you learn self talk techniques.If you talk yourself through your anger you'll be able to discover ways to deal with your anger as you see it through your eyes for the 1st time. Angriness is the direct effect of an incident. The individual dealing with anger might have been subject to disregard, abuse, bullies, and so forth. Those personal events were most likely not treated up front; rather the negative was left to build up to a point of blowup. Try to remember that the world doesn't center on you. The pain that trips your anger symptoms is frequently a result of your decision making.

For instance, the Net provider you pick continues making issues, like redirecting you when you're attempting to make a connection. This is enough to anger anybody. But, the company isn't centered on you. There's a breakdown in communicating on the company's part. Sure it's disturbing but it is a little fork in the road. No one is out to make your life awful. This should allow you to realize that we all experience bad instances, but how we cope with it is the key to success.

Anger frequently can result in rage and focuses on hostility. In most examples fury may overtake an individual fighting with anger. Anger may be a grave emotion that may lead to sinful measures. To some individuals with anger issues violence might be the answer to mending a problem but aggression only makes affairs worse. We have to look deep within ourselves and discover the instigating source of the blowup. Individuals are seldom upset because of words, actions, places or individuals. More often than not a mixed hatred has developed inside of them through a lot of years. Frequently the individual is lacking educational experience when we need maturity the most. Anger is nothing to play with when an individual looses their ability to sustain self-command. There are no confines to what their anger may do. When we get huffy we're consuming all of our energy and time on negative powers that commonly don't bear results. Utilizing anger to our benefit is a choice most individuals don't recognize. It commonly takes you on a rollercoaster of mental breakdown and verbal blowup. There are a lot of ways that anger devours our time and can detract from our quality of life. There's no need to take out your frustrations on other people, particularly your youngsters or your pets. If you discover yourself doing this frequently you ought to speak to your doctor about a depression screening and to talk about your options. We face problems daily like anger, prejudice, and crime. This sort of anger may only hurt individuals and occasionally in mass numbers. Hate crimes have overpowered our world. Exposing unrestrained anger only hurts yourself as well as other people. We have to discover a way to cope with anger on all levels to advance in life. Some of us determine it easier to deal with our issues in a suitable way while other people act out violently. In a sense, we all depend upon one another directly or indirectly. We may use anger positively and on the way to having a much richer life and meaningful life-style. At this stage, anger appears to rule the world. Since we're all involved with the violence that besets our system we all need to take the 1st step in coping with our emotions that induce anger and it will be beneficial to us all. Discover how to show patience to somebody you know that's dealing with an anger issue. Push positive thoughts and energy to keep anger from devouring your time. A different way to manage your anger and your time is to make sure of turning off your mind when you get concerned about the stressful things that life throws at you. Tell a friend about the concern and cares you have and tell them about your inclinations. Ask them to speak to you about it. It's truly nice to have a shoulder to lean against and an ear to vent to. This is a good strategy to utilize when you're trying to avoid anger attacks.

Chapter 6:

Taking Charge of Your Anger

Synopsis

The beginning thing you'll need to do when attempting to mend your anger issues is to evaluate the level of anger you have. Measuring your thoughts and emotions will lead you to the answers to your issues.

Command It

When your emotions are jeopardized you might be prone to flare up. In some cases, it may lead to acting irrational. When you're assessing the issue you're studying the level of the problem, the resolution to mend the problem, and the problem's significance. Assessing your problem slows the mind down so that it may think before it acts. If you lack in this region, rehearsing now would be a great idea.

If you leave anger to hang around for too long it may lead to true problems. You'll never wander from course of life's success journey by assessing your life and making the correct decisions from the beginning. Don't forget that issues will arrive and you have to face them head on. You are able to cope with your anger easily by maintaining a good outlook on life. There's no mountain you can't cross when you can see your path out of any jam. To cross a mountain you require a technique, self-confidence and hope to last through the path to recovery. Looking on life as a rollercoaster ride may be beneficial to any situation. There will be protrusions along the way. Honestly, it's an intense ride that's challenging as well as energizing. By challenging your potentiality and evaluating your anger you can take charge of any rocky spot. Again, nearly all of our troubles stem from our personal decisions and discovering how to stop and think prior to making rash decisions will lessen the troubles along the road of life. If you ever get the impression that you're losing control take a minute to stop and think. Ahead of you is a decision to be made and the correct way to deal with the issue. There's only one way that anger turns useful, that's when you're in a high-risk situation and there's no exit. It's possible to consider anger as either a beneficial or foul source knowing that it may benefit or lead to major issues in life. No one ever stated dealing with anger is simple. Individuals are forever dealing with issues that may result in anger. It's how you cope with it that's the secret for most to defeat their problems. There isn't a single individual on Earth that's never been mad at some point. Anger is something we all cope with. Now let's see all the aspects of a person's anger. Many individuals in this creation have issues with anger. Here are a few ideas to help you cope with your anger:

If you lie, cheat, steal, commit any wickedness, own it. Make certain you've no issue admitting your defects, as this will add to your self value and mutual respect.

Find something that calms you down. Exercise, sports, walk in the park, diaries, there are answers for everybody to deal with their own anger, but it's a personal decision. Pick what you like most. Visit acquaintances and loved ones. Redirect your feelings and vigor. Find additional ways to transmit your anger into productive forms. Talk to somebody about how you're feeling. Talk to your physician if anger is a true problem for you. You'll want to know if it's a mental issue for you or not. This way you are able to fix it easier.

Most anger problems have been with you your entire life. You might need some serious counseling to help repair the problem. Stand back from trouble. Try and help somebody every chance you get. This will add self-esteem. There's nothing better than feeling pleased with yourself. Admitting that you've a problem may also help. Telling your acquaintances and loved ones that you need support will ensure that somebody will always be there when you need them. Stand back from alcohol at any cost. It may fuel the fire of anger you might have inside. There's no way to tell how you'll behave when you're intoxicated. You don't want to harm anybody when you're sober, but you might end up doing it after you've had some to drink.

Wrapping Up

Many people with anger issues have realized that it's connected with alcohol and/or drugs directly. You might be surprised to discover that it may be a tremendous help in your effort away from anger. Drinking causes emotions to flash and conversations on touchy subjects to come up. You never know what you might say to offend another individual with an anger disease. Stand back from alcohol if you want to have a chance of recuperating.

In reviewing the source of our anger it will help us to determine the answers we left out while our emotions had control. Emotions are our inventory and may control our sadness, joy and above all anger. Having trouble managing your emotions may cause you to suffer from anxiety, depressions and blowups.

Solutions include putting down your emotions, working out your frustrations in the gymnasium, or finding your own way of doctoring your issues. Either of these things will work for you, but you have to make certain it's a personal gain. If you pick something to help you out with anger it must be something you like and something that works for you. Everybody is different. If the person doesn't discover a way to command the emotions that bring on anger flare-ups, anger will most likely overcome them.

Vitamin C and Vitamin B Complex have been utilized for years to enhance the mind and help the patient deal with stress. Throughout this book you've started to find out many ways to cope with anger and grab a hold of your anger. Like:

- Center on littler tasks at a time
- Slowly move forward to bigger goals when you're ready
- Learn to loosen up
- Write your issues down
- Take deep breaths when required
- Analyze your issues
- Exercise and yoga are great for unwinding your mind and body

- Take your time altering your issues
- Baby yourself
- Remind yourself daily you're moving towards recovery
- Keep your tension level low
- Practice what you preach to your youngsters
- Inform your acquaintances and family so they know about your problem and how they may help you through it
- Self help groups
- Talk to your physician if nothing is helping your problem

8892625R00024

Printed in Great Britain
by Amazon.co.uk, Ltd.,
Marston Gate.